*Grateful appreciation goes to TANDAVA
and ALURA in which several of THE OLD WAYS poems
first appeared. THE OLD WAYS won the Poet-Hunt
competition at Schoolcraft College in 1985.
They were published in revised form in its entirety
in THE MACGUFFIN and were nominated for a
Pushcart Prize in 1988.*

Copyright © 1991 by Kathleen Ripley Leo

ISBN: 0-941543-01-3

THE OLD WAYS

Kathleen Ripley Leo

SUN DOG PRESS
Northville, Michigan

Sun Dog Chapbooks
#1 of a series

II.

We children perched on angel-legged iron benches
under an oil painting of white callas and silver candelabra.
Our card tables were enveloped in white linen
as if a second skin wrapped us tight.
We listened to the adults at the mahogany table,
to their mutterings, their shouts,
their slips of the tongue into English
when their language was not enough.
We gaped as their fists jabbed the air,
or pounded and pooled on the table.
Chins jutted from white collared necks.
Women's voices slit men's low growls.
A violin in the background tore the landscape apart.
Tuya pravda. They were unbeatable.

Grandmother ladled out her noodles and soup.
Back and forth she'd wander filling bowls.
The soup ladle threaded through their debating
or dueling, or was it their way of making love?
Kielbasa, cwikla, pierogis and roasted chicken.
Steaming bowls on the linen cloth.
We children kept to the card tables, just out of reach.
Dobrezje, dobrezje, don't pay any attention, they said.

I.

We children listened to their words boom out,
Polish or Ukrainian or some mix,
words that seemed mangled and flattened
as though a wringer washer like my grandmother's
could yank these words from their tongues,
encode the meaning, and crush
everything they didn't want us to know.

They spoke little of this language to us,
so it took time to figure out who was mad at whom,
and the price of things they bought.
We half-understood some family stories,
their secrets, their dreams,
and that somewhere, the old country
where my grandparents, mother, aunt, uncle,
and all the outcast neighbors had come from.
What did they leave behind?
Don't think about it, they said.

IV.

My grandmother's hands could sculpt ponczki,
chisel mountains of dough and slap out
small circles for pierogis. She flattened
huge sheets for noodles and cooked great
pans of borscht and czarnina on the kitchen stove,
wrung the necks of fat hens,
sliced noodles, tender nipples of dough.

She drew up her flour to a tall cone,
funneled it with eggs and salty water,
gathered into the dough, and like an ocean wave, she kneaded it
back and forth, her arms and shape given up to it.
She taught me to roll up half dried sheets of dough
after they hung like crisp linens over front room chairs.
Each day she made it fresh, folded it up fat and long,
took her knife and sliced it into pieces for the soup.

III.

Moja zlota dzievczynka,
No one needs to know, she said.
One day I found out where they had come from.
My grandmother pointed quickly to a wooden globe
hoping no one else would see or overhear.
Europe--they had come from Europe,
and I was to tell no one.

V.

The day she bought her silver knife
the knifeman suddenly turned up in our basement.
His shadow dropped ahead of him
off the dark walls of the first floor landing.

Turkeys fattened up in the coal room,
cackled and echoed the knocking of her wringer.
She teased folds of embroidered tablecloth
into the tight lips of the wringer.
I thought her fingers would be crushed.

I imagined she was always risking her life,
if not in the wringer, it was cutting bread--
the big loaf on her breast
and the knife drifting toward her--
or when she sliced her noodles, I waited
for blood from her fingertips
to squeeze over the thick sheaf of rolled up dough.

The knifeman swiped the air with his knives
so she bought the one with the carved handle.
Perhaps it was the one she wanted anyway.
She told me, "Katje, no one should know,
don't tell anyone we bought it in the basement.
The kitchen is the place to buy knives,
but *stoĺe* good silver, heavy,
for bread or roast, good to slice soup noodles."

VI.

Her kitchen was the place she skinned rabbits.
Meat simmered in the beet soup, gravy red and thick.
This was the place she dressed poultry,
plucked feathers as the skin winced,
pink wings shivered against the white sink.
She dragged entrails out of dark cavities,
bloody worms trailed off her fingers
as she cupped a yolk and showed it to me,
"See, Kajte, this chicken was going to have babies."

The kitchen was the place Aunt Olga
ate corn out of the pot, sucking juice from the cobs.
How small the kernels and how large her breasts.
"There are no bones in breasts," she answered.
I touched the sides of them, there are no bones.

The kitchen was the place my grandmother sorted
white shirts, dark pants, white underwear,
rubbing out stains with a shudder.
"Katje, being with a man is one step in hell.
The best is, know everything, then forget it."

It was also the place grandfather drank,
his shot and a beer poured ready for him.
In the old country he sang tenor in operattas.
Now he sang to furnaces he repaired on a night-job,
through the welded pipes and angel-legged tables
he tooled at his day-job. Once he made her sit
in the middle of the room while he yelled
about something in their language. She cupped
her chin like the yolk, her other hand
picked at her skirt, but she did not wince.

VII.

Grandfather Mikhail was made of muscle
and gristle, and his legs were knotty with veins.
He had shoulders like a bull
and like a bull, hairs tufted his head.
He rubbed the sweat back from his forehead,
the passing of a decade in each swipe.
Oy yoy yoy yoy yoy
he'd say to me, a child, as he patted my rump.

Difficult to believe his wife with a child tugging at her
followed him like a bestial blessing to the new world,
had to track him down when he changed his name
and fled to Ottawa.

Hired killers he said were after him,
hired killers from the old country,
here to assassinate Austrian throne pretenders.
Already they tried to kill, twice tried to kill,
his cousin in Chicago.

Never mind the new woman.
A convenience he called her.

VIII.

Boris, a friend of Mikhail,
came on Sundays for a bowl of borscht
or a drink. They passed the time
in their language, played pinochle
these big men, their brown trousers big
and white shirts spread out,
They spat laughter and *Nazdrowies* under our pear tree,
laughter like the whack of croquet mallets.
We played in the side yard,
our house the only one in the neighborhood
with a double yard.

Sometime in the late afternoon,
from the darkened basement landing,
Boris called to us little girls, one at a time.
His hat still covered his bald head,
shaded a toothless mouth,
top window sunlight protected him in shadows.
A fifty cent piece shone in the center
of his palm, his hand stretched out to me,
like a star, five points to the light.

"Here, Kajte, come take it, for ice cream.
Don't be afraid," he called.
I forgot about the darkness,
the shadows. "Where is it,
give it to me, yes, I want ice cream."

He would pick me up and the smell of drink
was comfortable. His mouth was slippery
over mine, and four times as large.

I saved my fifty cent pieces, planted them
in the spider plants under the catalpa tree.
It was grandmother's pride.
On 42nd St. and Archer Ave.,
there was not another one like it she'd say,
maybe not in all of Chicago.

IX.

In the old country, Uncle Bruno grabbed his wife,
ripped off her skirts, tied her to a tree, and beat her.
She hung there until some men, in passing,
cut her down. Later these same men
caught Bruno, for her.

When I met him he was old and silent,
there was no wife.
His clothes were made of brown gabardine.
Old socks, membranes of beige around his ankles.
Rumors about him
sifted through the words they didn't teach us.

He would sit through family gatherings
and watch us children play.
One Christmas he let us open his presents.
He sat in his chair, torn paper
strewn on his lap and arms,
and his eyes bulged as if he saw his blood
popping out of his skin.

It didn't surprise me sometime later
when he died of cancer, I had heard he'd had it
once before, part of his upper lip
had been cut away.
It's from pipe smoking, they said.

X.

The day the war ended
Uncle Pieter stepped out
of the concentration camp,

those days collapsed to a dank breath.
He relished the defeat.
He would go back to his village in Poland

with the ring taken from the soldier
he had served, and it would be a present
for his wife, for Anna.

Her distant fragrance still sought him,
her laughter was a moon captured in two shells.
He opened it at night in his secret heart.

Pieter walked home across the terrain
of two countries,
the rubble of five years.

Anna stepped into the sunlight,
her hair in ribbons, and the village
was preparing a feast.

The two lovers did not
recognize each other, at first,
that day Pieter returned to Anna,

but he knew her silences as if it were
yesterday, and the marriage ribbons
she wore as she had when they married.

The green and yellow ribbons she wore
that very day, thinking him,
those five long years, dead.

XI.

She said never talk with strangers,
if one tries to grab you, jump up and down,
wave to some lady you don't know, and say,
"Oh, hi, Aunt Olga. Here I am."
This worked once, for Aunt Olga.

She sent me to the corner store,
a note and money in my hand.
I would walk, fearful of being stolen.
Even at home I was certain
some stranger hid under the bed,
and she was surprised to find me
under the covers, but she was very pleased,
I was smart enough to hide.

XII.

At the corner store I once complained
how stale the carmels were, and old.
My friends told me how rude it was,
to say the carmel was stale--
tasted stale and hard.
It made the owner feel bad.
But, did they ever hear my grandmother
talk in broken English--her pearls and riding habit
and embroidery in the old country.
My aunt's boyfriends and roses in the new country.
Did she make anyone else a braided velvet coat,
and doll clothes like ball gowns,
tell anyone else, never lose your ideals.
Couldn't someone at least make a good carmel,
the light brown circle fresh and stubborn,
the fat white sugar center enthroned.

The owner of the corner store was a man with red eyes,
who looked at me suspiciously.
When he took down a cereal box,
his hook at times stuck to the box.
Corn flakes and farina would fall on the butcher counter
like a pile of stars for sale.
To get what I had come in for--
he had to go in the back for it,
just enough time for me to take a mint.
A foil wrapping never quite hides the smell of mint.

It was like my grandmother's handbag,
it always hid a peppermint for my tongue.
How could the man with the red eyes ever know--
the smell of mint fills the universe.

*Printed February 1991 in Northville for
Sun Dog Press. Design by Allen Berlinski.
Text set in New Century Schoolbook.
There are 250 trade copies;
50 copies have screen printed covers on
archival handmade paper from Dieu Donne' Papermill,
were handbound in wraps,
and have been numbered & signed by the author.*